RHYTHM, CONTENT & FLAVOR

VICTOR HERNANDEZ CRUZ

ARTE
PUBLICO
PRESS

a grant from the National
ency.

Arte Publico Press
University of Houston
Houston, Texas   77204-3784

Cruz, Victor Hernández, 1949-
    Rhythm, content & flavor: new and selected poems /
Victor Hernández Cruz.
        p.   cm.
        ISBN 0-934770-93-X : $8.00
        I. Title. II. Title: Rhythm, content and flavor
    PS3553.R8R47 1988
    811'.54--dc19   89-14542
                                      CIP

Printed in the United States of America

Para mi hija

Rosa-Luz Kattie-Kairi

"AscaracaristikiscaristikiscaristikiscaracatisAscaracatiski
tiscatiskitiscatiskitisAscaracatiskitiscatiskitiscarakatis."

Mon Rivera

El trabalengua
de Puerto Rico

CONTENTS

Introduction

Rhythm, content and flavor presents selections from Victor Hernández Cruz's four previous books and includes a new work in its entirety: *Islandis: The Age of Seashells.*

When Random House issued the poetic works of a New York Puerto Rican prodigy in *Snaps* (1968), it was fully aware of the originality, power and clarity of vision in the young poet's snapshots of life in the urban ghetto. The Random House editors, while respectful of Cruz's diction--which was apparently nurtured in black English and popular music--and his irreverence for some of the formalities of grammar and style, probably did not realize that they were launching a life-long journey, a profound search for the sense in sound--all sound--and for the source of all poetry and music. Not merely a jazz poet or a Puerto Rican poet or a black poet or a ghetto poet--as many of his first critics tried to pigeon-hole him--as his career progressed it became apparent that Hernández Cruz was the poetic imagination personified, free to muster all of the resources of two languages, the sounds and images of many cultures--including the cultures of Asia and Africa--the improvizational impulse of jazz, the orality of street poets, the imagism of hieroglyphic painters, the magic of shamans, the wonder and fresh vision of children.

What coalesces the images of Victor Hernández Cruz's first four books--*Snaps* (1968), *Mainland* (1973), *Tropicalization* (1976) and *By Lingual Wholes* (1982)-- is the dominant presence of the poet himself and the beloved pulsating rhythm of *salsa* music, the rhythm which carries the poet back to his African and Indian roots. *Salsa* soul music energizes his poetry into a revolutionary literary document and an affirmation of his Puerto Rican culture. Hernández Cruz conceives of poetry as music and believes in the power of poetry and music to strenghten people and bring about social change. *Snaps* defines Hernández Cruz's art, while *Mainland* is a poetic odyssey through the United States that eventually leads back to the source, the mother of his music and poetry: Borinquen. *Tropicalization* is a renewed vision of the United States as a surrealistically transformed society, which slowly, magically is metamorphosing its identity to the beat of the Hispanic presence within. *By Lingual Wholes* is Hernández Cruz's attempt to merge and contrast the sound and significance of two languages and cultures. The fusing at times takes the form of his whimsical transliterations and tongue-in-cheek translations (*frenesí*-friend in C, friend in me) and other times is a serious assertion of the loss of meaning in translation, the loss of poetry and power in translation:

> *This is all in Spanish and something is being lost in the translation like you lose your natural color when you leave a tropical country and come to the city ...*

In *By Lingual Wholes*, a slower paced book, relying more on the melodic *bolero* rather than the hotter *salsa*, the more pensive Hernández Cruz declares in the title and in his gestures to Puerto Rican folk culture on the island and mainland that there is a wholeness, not a schizoid separation, in living in and creating from two languages and cultures. And in "Art This," the source of the art, the artistry for the poet and the people, is in not having to translate; it is in comprehending, communing, unifying with the source and the godhead through the sound and the music directly without recognizing linguistic or cultural barriers.

Islandis: The Age of Seashells is a return to the theme touched upon in *Mainland* and *Tropicalization* of Puerto Rico as the source of music and knowledge. Puerto Rico, like the lost island of Atlantis, with its flowing tropical breezes and ocean currents, creates a music like, in the Renaissance, was created by the heavenly spheres revolving around the earth. As in all of his works, Victor Hernández Cruz re-defines poetry as *la salsa de Dios*; God is the origination of all poetry and music; poetry is God's music.

Nicolás Kanellos
Publisher, Arte Publico Press

SNAPS

1967-1969

today is a day of great joy

when they stop poems
in the mail & clap
their hands & dance to
them

when women become pregnant
by the side of poems
the strongest sounds making
the river go along

it is a great day

as poems fall down to
movie crowds in restaurants
in bars

when poems start to
knock down walls to
choke politicians
when poems scream &
begin to break the air

that is the time of
true poets that is
the time of greatness

a true poet aiming
poems & watching things
fall to the ground

it is a great day

going uptown to visit miriam

on the train
old ladies playing football
going for empty seats

very funny persons

the train riders
                are silly people
                i am a train rider

but no one knows where i am
going to take this train

to take this train
to take this train

the ladies   read popular
paperback   because they
are popular   they get off
at 42 to change for the
westside line   or off
59 for the department store

the train pulls in & out
the white walls   dark-
ness   white walls   dark-
ness

ladies looking up   i
wonder where they going
the dentist   pick up
husband pick up wife
pick up kids
pick up? grass?
to library   to museum
to laundromat   to school

but no one knows where i am
going to take this train

to take this train

to visit miriam
to visit miriam

& to kiss her
on the cheek
& hope i don't
see sonia on the
street

But no one knows where i'm taking
this train
taking this train
to visit miriam.

energy

is
red beans
ray barretto
banging away
steam out the
radio
the five-stair
steps
is mofongo
cuchifrito stand
outside down
the avenue
that long hill
of a block
before the train
is pacheco
playing with
bleeding
blue lips

Cities
(moved singing/laughing/feeling/
talking/dancing)

1
subway in
subway out
grove street
nine blocks
fifth ward
downtown
jersey city
the avenue
emtpy & lit
the store owner
hanging out
the doors
making legal
robberies.

2
we trust
the stairs
of a building
& they are
not even ours.

3
new projects
elevators
highways
snow
pot & hashish
stereo music
pucho & the latin
soul brothers
disturb
anglo-saxon
middle-class
loving
americans.

4
washington st.
the kind of party
you have to take
your hanky out
a bag of smoke
with a nail
inside
i mean/shit
i've seen a whole
lot of shit pass
for grass
but no nail.

5
together
drag your feet
in the snow
it's new year's
they say.

6
the kidney foundation
wants more money
& if you eat cheerios
you'll have power
so says the t.v.
that woke me up.

7
central
dance-hall
musicians
smoke before
they come out
the red exit
sign
the blue lights
girls with
black leather
pants
sweet
talk
&
sweat.

8
little cousins
play on your
fingers & head
& want kisses
before you leave.

9
they had women
in their pockets
a story of the
harbor
clowns come to town
hollering
they kick they ass

shit like that.

latin & soul

for Joe Bataan

1
some waves
                a wave of now
                              a trombone speaking to you
a piano is trying to break a molecule
is trying to lift the stage into orbit
around the red spotlights

a shadow
the shadow   of dancers
dancers   they are dancing   falling
out that space   made for dancing

they should dance
on the tables   they should
dance inside of their drinks
they should dance on the
ceiling they should dance/dance

the universes
leaning-moving
                we are traveling

where are we going
if we only knew

with this rhythm   with
this banging   with   fire
with this   all   this
my god i wonder   where are we going
              sink into a room full of laughter
              full of happiness   full of life
              those dancers
              the dancers
                    are clapping their hands
                    stomping their feet

hold back them tears

                              all those sentimental stories
cooked uptown   if you can   hold it for after

we are going
                    away-away-away
                    beyond these wooden tables
                    beyond these red lights
                    beyond these rugs & paper
                    walls   beyond   way past
                    i mean way past them clouds
                    over the buildings   over the
                    rivers   over towns   over cities
                    like on rails   but faster   like
                    a train   but smoother
                    away past stars
                    bursting with drums.

      2
      a sudden misunderstanding
                          a cloud
                          full of grayness
      a body thru a store window
                          a hand reaching
                          into the back
                          pocket
      a scream
                    a piano is talking to you
                    thru all this
                    why don't you answer it.

descarga en cueros

louie was dragging his legs on the floor
at the bar people's drinks flew out they hands
the vibrations knocked people to the floor / & the
lights began to bust / & the floor to crack
it started raining sweat & drinks / people on top
of tables / or coming out of all kinds of holes / the sound
engineer went home / a wall fell down & the place opened
up to the street / people ran & whistled / & laughed
almost choking themselves / daisy put her ears in her
pockets / carlos' head was leaning against a wall / sally
was crying & yelling O my god / the floor began to rock
people fell off the balcony / t.p. was smiling / his face
ready to rip / o.k. you win / hands in the air ready to
fly / heads outside beyond the buildings.

Megalopolis

(megalopolis--is urban sprawl--as from
Boston to N.Y.C., Philly, Washington,
D.C., the cities run into each other)

highway of blood / volkswagens crushed up
against trees
it's a nice highway, ain't it, man
colorful / it'll take you there
will get there round eight with corns on
your ass   from sitting
turn the radio on & listen /   no
turn the shit off
let those lights & trees & rocks
talk / going by / go by   just sit
back / we / we go into towns /   sailing the
east coast / westside drive   far-off
buildings look like castles / the kind
dracula flies out of / new england of houses
& fresh butter / you are leaving the nice
section now   no more woods / into rundown
overpopulated areas, low income / concrete walls
of amercia / a poet trying to start riots /
arrested with bombs in pockets / conspiracy
to destroy america / america/ united states /
such a simple thing / lawrence welk-reader's
digest ladies news big hair styles with all
that spray to hold it / billboards of the high-
way are singing lies / & as we sail we under-
stand things bettter / the night of the buildings
we overhead flying by / singing magic words
of our ancestors.

The Eye
Uptown & Downtown
(three days)

1
good things always happen
for instance
cats jump from building
to building in silence.
2
the dope on the
corner moves slowly
junkies dance the
boogaloo.
3
sleeper's head
is crushed against
the concrete
blood stains his ears.
4
one dice weighs
more than the other
knifes went thru space.
5
who knew
who stole
their bullshit
from their lips.
6
the long line
turns
slowly moves
inside.
7
buildings talk spanish
at night.
8
she had everything
she hated.
9
people walk the wall

they let them walk
the water
do the concrete pull.
10
his things are
wherever he wants them
to be
into any street
full.
11
the soft summer wind
has the smell of the
building on the corner.
12
junkies rob their mothers.
13
CURA CURA CURA
BAILA BOOGALOO.
14
watch the clothes burn
& wonder who put it on fire.
15
let the sun
send all it
wants
& we love it.
16
the piano lost its
teeth
the trombone fell apart
the conga drifted.
17
madison is good way
downtown
& way uptown
fuck the middle.
18
the lexington train
broke down.
19
a parade
of smokes
didn't get far.

20
everyone falls asleep
the radio plays memories
glass falls to the floor
the window left open
the lights make shapes
the rooftops hold hands.
21
trees get in the way
of dumb ladies sticking
out of windows.
22
everyday you turn
& turn again
it gets brighter
peep-peep-peep.
23
the stairs are full of holes
one big hole
no stairs.
24
stop sending the
wire downtown
stop talking
& do the rough ride.
25
BANG BANG.
26
small talk
turns into
gutter stomp.
27
the garbage truck
rolled over his ears.
28
what time is the
lame session over.
29
hospitals full with death
pigs
& lonely nurses.
30
death everywhere
coat cut

throat slit
smash against a wall
blood
wallet three feet away
empty.
31
the stories came
this happened
in this manner
which ever
ways.
32
slow the city up
watch
let it all hang out.

spirits

half of his
body hung in
the air
they said it was
magic   a secret
between me & the man
it was no magic that was
in the air   it was no trick
an old lady an old   old lady who
saw the windows open   the wind raising the
curtains   footsteps in an empty room
a young man who saw a t.v. go flying into the
air   a dying lady got up & walked & sang
sudden loss of weight   sudden accident   a car
rolling over a head   a building falling
bad luck   magic.

go after them as they get lost to turn the corner & snag
one   flowers   odors   candles   light candles   morning
noise   papers flying.
a hand thru a wall
is no joke   a mind
going mad at a days
time   so wide
so wide spread
an escape
who escapes   who
runs   run where
from   what from
who   a silence
the clouds over
the buildings the
odor in the halls
no one runs
no place to run
no place to hide
traveling   a fast

traveler   a signal
a place   the strange
way the walls start
to act   you say
you say you saw
nothing moving there
you deny a head
a head hiding   behind
the curtains   take
another look
a storm reported

only on your street
someone with grade A
health found dead of
a strange disease
a bad cold
a box found
full of nails
& flowers
names & statues
water sitting under
the beds   blood
falling out of pictures
a flower   burning under
the bed
a lady dressed in
white   flying away
from the roof
waving her hands
for you to follow
you have a bad cold

there is no medicine
there is no cure
there is only a fear
a hope   a waiting
till the spirits
come to our rescue
to your funerals

all the third world
sees spirits &
they talk to them
they are our friends.

RITMO 1

everybody passed the drummer / drummers in the park
drummers in the sky /

> we went up six flights
> looking down at garages
> & stores & listening to
> drums / all the way from
> the park / all the way from
> the sky

everybody
staring out / riding the roofs / look at the lights
of palisades / the round circles in the black sky
float all the way to the edge of the park / standing
by the river   the blue lights & red lights of
commerce / the windows of brooklyn /

> monk dropped his glass
> on someone's head / cause
> that's what he wanted to
> do / all over a shirt / & what
> about it

everybody
hanging on like clothes on the line / drummers
writing poems in the sky / drummers   pulling off
their shirts / the trees echo the passages / & we on
the roof quietly resting / looking at summer / at
the lights that the city creates / the airplanes
shoot by   over highways   & rivers /

everybody
passed by the drummers / roof & windows over
head & eyes on fire

MAINLAND

1972-1973

*Sometimes, from its hidden hoarse-voiced
high sea, from those unexplored distances,
come echoes so vague that they lose themselves
like swooning waves on an immobile coast
of mists and silence. They are messages that
reach us in desperation from unknown depths
of these secret dramas; cries for help, voices,
moans like those from a huge ship that is
being wrecked in the distance.*

Luis Palés Matos

En la Casa de Verta

For Verta Mae Grosvenor

for on monday in 1969   on the streets
was diamonds   downtown society
bodegas one right after the other
avocado and tomato juice   space
ships parked in front of Verta's house
sparkling yellow metal   with stickers
from venus Airlines   Moon Shuttle
Jupiter Car Service   Mars Helicopter
and all on Monday by a bridge   1969
year of the Rooster   hot sauce
street beans
caribbean rice on the fire
with african juice warming
the centuries and centuries
of sea exploration and mixing

here we all are in Verta's
soul space kitchen
taking off

Blue Boat

People walking down the street
like they're on their way to the clouds
or somewhere higher
Walking in silence
I listen to a thousand windows
lift themselves open
Out comes a million rhythmic
songs
Out comes a cup of water
Perhaps a mirror broke
Or someone is cleaning the house
Why in January cold you look
toward God's house with burning eyes
Why in July you skip in the street
In a light dress covering your knees
and your wind is like an elephant's
When one turns to look at the storm
All they see is you dancing by
Just a little bit.

And this is just a fragment of this
Massive day
And it is still early
and most of the noise is not here yet
All of you
What it is today
that I go out and can't help
but laugh every time I take three steps
There is always something popping
from the mad
Why is it that you walk down
the streets like you're going to heaven
on a blue boat
On a blue boat full of songs
On a blue boat full of heads

leaning comfortably back
With a mambo that has a thousand trumpets
and 400 timbales
It is the secret guide of the navigator
who sits in his room in the blue boat
The blue boat that is this day.

Discovery

Watching a thousand smiles
that were full of sadness
standing in a wall
all sideways
My ears are the walls
No one can see me there
I am quiet
Still
Like the owls who sit atop
telephone polls

The traffic between
the walls
Those smiles that come
and go
Those darkened whiskers
suspended in the air
Those souls
Spirits
Coming from one thing
and going to another
but belonging nowhere

The walls breathe
My ears are hung like
blankets
My legs disappear into the
roof
My hands touch the building
next door
I swing from the walls
to the ceilings
No one hears me

I watch a yellow dress
that floats across
the rooms and stares

out of the windows
The Saints walk through
the walls
San Martín has a whole bowl
of grapes sitting on
the altar
he eats one every time
he walks by

Words come out of the rooms
like millions of fire crackers
They slam
Dance against the walls

On a clear Jupiter
The sun enters
Works its way in
Through the parted curtains
It moves inside the yellow
dress that hangs on
Yolanda

So
if you see a yellow dress
flying
Looking down on those
who walk the earth
with borrowed shoes
It's only Yolanda
cooking food
In through the door
and out through
the roof

My ears are the walls
And they hear it all
The yellow dress
It sometimes slips
and falls
Way in there
Where a smile

is six hundred miles
Way in there
where the Indians went to.

Berkeley/Over

Bird wings over the bay
Electronic bombs below
Waves talking to la moon
A town of philosophical habits
Cold turkey would kill it
So it just sits and cops
Everyday.

An empire of hidden houses
Behind the green wall of the hills
Staring down into the flats
Eyes looking for the airport
Where are the birds?

In the University a parade of sounds
Light show Music and Gowns
Talking walking
One day
When the sun came after the rain
Burgundy Almadén
A bit for San Pedro
The rest for the music.

The place had grown many
Creators from across the land
Some sit high up on the sides
of hills
Others walk miles just to visit.

When the Monsoon came
And some found nothing to do
But stare at candles

The house on Grove Street
Was the secret meeting place
For those who wanted to hear
the rhythms
Pure.

Part Three

Para Roberto Vargas

Red falcon / 4 in the morning
                5 in the morning
daylight whistles
and R.V. driving his car
down San Fra himalayas
his eyes bouncing around
the corners for somewhere
to go

We join the feast in colorful
three massive rooms
somewhere on a deserted street
blown hippy its stand against
walls
science pictures splashed against
floor and ceiling
a little dot show
nervous fingers change slides
and press down the switch
of many bulbs

We notice the air changes colors
We move into other rooms
way back in a closet full of sofas
An international conference is held
Rubén Darío comes by way of R.V.
fingernails as he pointed to a fact
that ran out of the building
It became lies and poems
short stories sneaking from the
room next door
We picked up and dragged ourselves
to the red rolls royce parked
horizontal on a one way street

We turned spiral hills
maneuvers guided by forces
outside the red coach
                    smiling and singing
louder than the coming earthquake
when it was very early
we ate under the silver sky
of Rubén Darío's parlors

Part Four

on 22nd and folsom
pacific ocean fish   boiling
far away and getting farther
a mean ice breeze sneaks upon
the city   makes everyone
speed up
when there is nothing to do
and the walls of the top floor
half a house no longer can
hold an urge to fly somewhere
and when lips have been pressed
together for three nights
walking around   studying hills
and wondering what 3,000 miles
away is like   after turning
down folsom of this west coast
city   head for the bay
looking for some loud beings
to show on the screen
at the edge of the nation
counting back on the population
and rows of homes   asleep
standing on the   last breath
of the town action
the moon she comes down
and spreads her
legs wide.

The Sounds of Colors

For Joe Overstreet

painting   #1
Go into
stars / the bluest
night in the world
the message loud & clear
red on purple
loud people of the
streets
turning into walls
as Chinese rockets
explode.

painting   #2
Brown & blue waves
of nature
floating ladies
laughing gringo boredom
above
butterflies that throw
bombs and Missiles
happy holiday
on canvas bright.

painting   #3
By the window
the owl sits in
yellow awareness
Filled with blackness
& love.

painting   #5
Purple orange blue
yellow walls
shooting shapes of

other worlds
geometric moons / spin
around its mysterious
creator.

From the Secrets I

What did the astronauts speak
When they rode the eagle's neck?

We know but will not tell
Silly how you move thousands
of years / to walk down Bronx
Avenues with tight red pants
And a smile as wide as the trucks
That pass you by

Thoughts in Spanish run through
the mind
The buildings speak broken English

Aquí
Where the birds landed
Drinking water from the streams
Cortez not knowing the sound of lips
That paraded up and down the hemisphere
Began the hunt of all these years

We know / but only know
In warm July somewhere dancing
Out from our eyes

Aquí

Land of tall cylinders   glass
between cement shining
Land of forgotten tongues
That surface from time to time
once on the Lexington Avenue local
moving into 103rd street
We meet Caquax sitting waiting for
the express   we turn to say hello
But he had gone into the wall
Bronx of walking streets

That turn into large strong eagles
The astronauts dance la plena
They dance till dawn / and fly all
day

Walking down Bronx Avenues
In red high yellow legs
Suddenly you forget where you are

And what time is it?

Las Vegas

In the brown Nevada desert
are your light bulbs
City of coins
George Washington and Lincoln
Slide into the slot machines
You are the stranger
That is too common
In the middle of nowhere
The poor middle aged men
Lose their hair
At the tables
Otherwise they'd have
Nothing to do.

Feast of the Guardian Saint

As if from the top
of mountains
Came voices
to modern wise men
Parading ina a circus-
like fiesta
In the plaza of Ceiba
Puerto Rico.

Who are the people
wrapped in cloth
With their blue bell bottoms
and the señoritas with their
beige hot pants
Ceiba from all the homes
that line your streets
Poured this mass of bodies
They put all their fires
on
All the colors for tonight
the height of la fiesta
of your guardian saint
All the colors for him
for he has watched well
over the mountains

Afternoons drive into nights
The machines turn
For twenty five cents
your body could go round
in circles for 8 minutes
Surrounded by multi-colored
light bulbs that go on and off
As the ride dips
low to the earth
and swings to the three
early stars

Shoots into space in circles
Spinning like the spin
of your still head Puerto Rico.

The business men who control
know nothing of the fine weather—
nor of themselves
Their windows are closed
and they no longer have hands
If they knew of their hands
and how good your body smells

They would encircle you
and kiss you all in the
greenness of your lomas—
Mayaqüez legs so good
And Orocovis your belly button
I sit here in the middle of the
plaza in Ceiba
Warming in the hottest fire
of las fiestas patronales
And I stare in the direction
Where I think is the closest
Mountain—
                    For it seems that
from the top of the mountains—
come voices.

Morena

If I found you in
Borinken
In a garden surrounded by rocks
I would slowly enter
And play with your hair

Like rhythm is your belly
It moves to this

Listen there is talk to this
la salsa de dios

As if the avenue
was the wet sand of the beach
Glide in memorial glances
Your eyes are like a strange
book
Walking in tune with flowers

In the garden of rocks
Some songs / some songs
So old for your eyes
For the tribe to grow
In the juice of your
belly.

You Gotta Have Your Tips on Fire

You never know who has your memory
in their drinks
In the cities that move into other
cities
Into other times
Ancient cities
You never know who wants to throw
you into that timeless space
Where you forget your name
And the face of the woman you love
Camará
You gotta have your tips on fire
You never know who has your thoughts
locked up in some small room
Wishing a thousand storms would
hit your doorway
Wishing you whirlwinds for paths
and hurricanes for the mornings
that open your days
You gotta have your tips on fire
Pana
Because they make doors out of pure
space
And you have to swing them open
So they know
You are around the wind
You are in the wind with your own
dance
You never know who stabs your
shadow full of holes
You gotta have your tips on fire
You never will be in the wrong place
For the universe will feel your heat
And arrange its dance on your head
There will be a Sun / Risa
On your lips

But
You gotta have your tips on fire
Carnal.

Los New Yorks

In the news that sails through the air
Like the shaking seeds of maracas
I find you out

Suena

You don't have to move here
Just stand on the corner
Everything will pass you by
Like a merry-go-round the red
bricks will swing past your eyes
They will melt
So   old
Will move out by themselves

Suena

I present you the tall skyscrapers
as merely huge palm trees with lights

Suena

The roaring of the trains is a fast
guaguancó
dance of the ages

Suena

Snow falls
Coconut chips galore
Take the train to Caguas
and the bus is only ten cents
to Aguas Buenas

Suena

A tropical wave settled here
And it is pulling the sun
with a romp
No one knows what to do

Suena

I am going home now
I am settled there with my fruits
Everything tastes good today
Even the ones that are grown here
Taste like they are from outer space
Walk y Suena
Do it strange
Los New Yorks.

The Man Who Came to the Last Floor

There was a Puerto Rican man who
came to New York
He came with a whole shopping bag
full of seeds strange to the big
city
He came and it was morning
and though many people thought the
sun was out this man wondered:
"Where is it"
"y el sol dónde está" he asked
himself
He went to one of the neighborhoods
and searched for an apartment
He found one in the large somewhere
of New York
with a window overlooking a busy avenue
It was the kind of somewhere that is
usually elevatorless
Somewhere near wall/less
stairless
But this man enjoyed the wide space
of the room with the window that
overlooked the avenue
There was plenty of space
looking out of the window
There is a direct path to heaven
he thought
A wideness in front of the living
room
It was the sixth floor so he lived
on top of everybody in the building
The last floor of the mountain
He took to staring out of his sixth
floor window
He was a familiar sight every day
From his window he saw legs that
walked all day

Short and skinny fat legs
Legs that belonged to many people
Legs that walk embraced with nylon socks
Legs that rode bareback
Legs that were swifter than others
Legs that were always hiding
Legs that always had to turn around
and look at the horizon
Legs that were just legs against
the grey of the cement
People with no legs
He saw everything hanging out
from his room
Big city anywhere and his smile
was as wide as the space in front of him

One day his dreams were invaded by spirits
People just saw him change
Change the way rice changes when it is
sitting on top of fire
All kinds of things started to happen
at the top of the mountain
Apartamento number 32
All kinds of smells started to come out
of apartamento number 32
All kinds of visitors started to come
to apartamento number 32
Wild looking ladies showed up
with large earings and bracelets
that jingled throughout the hallways
The neighborhood became rich in legend
One could write an encyclopedia if one
collected the rumors
But nothing bothered this man who was
on top of everybody's heads
He woke one day and put the shopping bag
full of seeds that he brought from the island
near the window
He said "para que aprovechen el fresco"
So that it can enjoy the fresh air
He left it there for a day

Taking air
Fresh air
Grey air
Wet air
The avenue air
The blue legs air
The teenagers who walked below
Their air
With their black hats with the red
bandana around them full of cocaine
That air
The heroin in the young girls that
moved slowly toward their local
high school
All the air from the outside
The shopping bag stood by the window
inhaling
police air
Bus air
Car wind
Gringo air
Big mountain city air anywhere
That day this man from Puerto Rico
had his three radios on at the same time
Music coming from anywhere
Each station was different
Music from anywhere everywhere

The following day the famous
outline of the man's head once again showed
up on the sixth floor window
This day he fell into song
and his head was in motion
No one recalls exactly at what point
in the song he started flinging the
seeds of tropical fruits down to
the earth
Down to the avenue of sowewhere big
city
But no one knew what he was doing
So all the folks just smiled

"El hombre está bien loco, algo le
cogió la cabeza"
The man is really crazy
something has taken his head
He began to throw out the last of the
Mango seeds
A policeman was walking down the avenue
and all of a sudden took off his hat
A mango seed landed nicely into his
curly hair
It somehow sailed into the man's
scalp
Deep into the grease of his curls
No one saw it
And the policeman didn't feel it
He put his hat on and walked away
The man from Puerto Rico
was singing another pretty song
His eyes were closed and his head waved.

Two weeks later the policeman felt
a bump coming out of his head
"Holy shit" he woke up telling his wife
one day
"this bump is getting so big I can't
put my hat on my head"
He took a day off and went to see his
doctor about his growing bump
The doctor looked at it and said
"it'll go away"
The bump didnt' go away
It went toward the sky
getting bigger each day
It began to take hold of his whole head
Every time he tried to comb his hair
all his hair would fall to the comb
One morning when the sun was really hot
his wife noticed a green leaf sticking
out from the tip of his bump
Another month passed and more and more
leaves started to show on this man's head

the highest leaf was now two feet above
his forehead
Surely he was going crazy he thought
He could not go to work with a mango
tree growing out of his head
It soon got to be five feet tall
and beautifully green
He had to sleep in the living room
His bedroom could no longer contain him
Weeks later a young mango showed up
hanging from a newly formed branch
"Now look at this" he told his wife
He had to drink a lot of water or he'd
get severe headaches
The more water he drank the bigger
the mango tree flourished over his head
The people of the somewhere city heard
about it in the evening news and there was
a line of thousands ringed around his
home
they all wanted to see the man who
had an exotic mango tree growing from
his skull
And there was nothing that could be done.

Everyone was surprised when they
saw the man who lived at the top of
the mountain come down with his shopping
bag and all his luggage
He told a few of his friends that
he was going back to Puerto Rico
When they asked him why he was going back
He told them that he didn't remember
ever leaving.

He said that his wife and children
were there waiting for him
The other day he noticed that he was
not on his island he said
almost singing
He danced toward the famous corner

and waved down a taxi
"El aire port" he said
He was going to the clouds
To the island
At the airport he picked up a newspaper
and was reading an article about a mango
tree
At least that's what he could make out of
the English
Qué cosa he said   Wao
Why write about a Mango tree
There're so many of them
and they are everywhere
They taste goooooooood
Cómo eh.

Aguadilla

We went to the house
Across the nation
The last people who went spoke of
the house being invisible from the
inside
Feel the house like the water
of Aguadilla
See the house like the walk of the
children in uniforms to school
We took the road by the ocean
We stopped into everything
By the stand where they sell cold
coconuts
The fried fish stand
*

We can go into the house and not go
*

It is a thousand years old
We practice Mambo till early morning
*

"You think it will rain before we get
to the banana trees?"
*

It stayed dry in Aguadilla
Chopping bananas all afternoon
*

The stove was burning
And the soft yellow smell of banana
*

And so the skin of a conga
also burns
Seven drums and three maracas
One güiro
14 bodies two blocks from the beach
*

Throwing rocks at mango trees
they fall into our hands

The weekend began on Thursday
and ended Monday night
*

The roosters are not given food
so they can grow mad and fight
In the round circle of the sport
Where the dollars fly into the
pockets of the strong
*

The house is light pink
Two floors and many widows
From the house we move to Mayagüez
The drums are sticking out of the
trunk
Drink beer under the sun
Sun melts the cans
*

The road back to Aguadilla
We meet up with caballeros
on horses
*

The house is still there
We see it from far
Forming from a small dot
We make out the pink sticking out
from all the greenness
Our caravan moves fast   including the
laughter
Including the fruits taken from the
lonely trees
From the house we hear the sea
Yemayá is blue and white
her song is deep within
*

We carry the drums on our backs
We go to the edge of the ocean
just where the water reaches
We turn around to look for the house
But it is not there
All we see is green rhythm coming
to eat us
Aguadilla   Sat.
                    Sun.   Summer 1971

67

TROPICALIZATION

1975-1976

"Cada loco con su tema"
> —Popular saying

Side 1

Me go in plane traffic
drinking Cola-Champaign la original
Floating
everytime I come to giant city
Hear tambores
inside of New Yorks flying
big legs
Yellow taxis flying glowing
through all streets
Where Con Edison beating the ground
Eternal repairs
Orange lights
Blue lights
Green lights
They should dig dig dig
All the way down
till they hear the voice
Of their mama.

Side 2

Out the window the window looking out
At you and him and them
Telling stories of the hot sun
walking around half naked
Suave moon   lifting skirts
your eyes inside the fibers
Tamarindo bitter sour sweet
no shoes going to the next enclave
of lights
In the mornings the subway
roars out of the inside of a
Red bean
the ice hugs the glass
Murray the K he says over radio
2 below zero outside.

Side 5

Hair rollers holding up her mind
They are called batteries in Spanish
Sign of hectic Saturday afternoon
Somewhere tonight electric hair will fly
Will wave to a piano
Will cry to some sad guitar

Side 12

Manhattan dance Latin
In Spanish to African rhythms
A language lesson
Without opening your mouth

Side 22

What you want is for the tiger to eat me
The one at Central Park
Loose in my dreams
What you want is for me to become like
the cold
February anyone
What you want is for that tiger to eat me
I won't close my eyes tonight
Hear the river
See the boats
Calculating at night
In the mornings
This is like living inside a refrigerator
trying to have thoughts
Wondering how lovely a woman's body is
through all those sweaters and coats
Is that the case
What you want is for the tiger to eat me
Knock knock
I bring you his bones

Side 24

Walk el cement
Where las chinas roll
illuminating my path
Through old streets
With ancient tales
Crawling up my feet
It is late
They say you gotta
Watch your step
On these loco streets
My purpose here is not that
Walking down the street
To see the chinas roll

Side 25

Silver moon carry me home in your arms
I have nothing on me
Not a penny not a gun
All the sleepy windows
That I see your face in
It is late
And it's such a long way
Greet me at the next corner
Or throw me a subway token

Side 27

So many windows have lost
their power to hold back the wind
Millions of bricks getting tired
And sick beyond medicine
Dragging to the next decade
Marine Tiger who didn't eat
Millions of hands
Shirts and blouses
Nostrils how many
Shoes millions
How many little buttons in New
York
Little dimes in little corners
How many notebooks and pictures
Hanging on tanto walls
Sideways y upside dowm
Left ways alley ways right ways
Do you know the 7 deadly sins
Back ways or front ways
Choo Choo loco motives for all
this population holocaust
STOP
Disappearing and melting
Appearing vanishing
My body dressed in orange
In purple blues and turquoise
Wake up all the pirates
and their women
La danza of words tonight
The only thing that can hold truth
Among these ten trillion windows
of light

Side 29

Notary publics are important community freaks
They wear gold teeth and have all their cavities filled
Their high school graduation ring   is the biggest in the
Neighborhood   It is an important job what they do
The rubber stamp weighs two ounces   They pick it up
and carry it over the face of white paper in front
of them and cli-tin—once again you have to pay

Side 32

I am glad that I am not one of those
Big Con Edison pipes that sits by the
River crying smoke
I am glad that I am not the doorknob
Of a police car patrolling the Lower
East Side
How cool I am not a subway token
That has been lost and is sitting
Quietly and lonely by the edge of
A building on 47th Street
I am nothing and no one
I am the possibility of everything
I am a man in this crazy city
I am a door and a glass of water
I am a guitar string cutting through the
Smog
Vibrating and bringing morning
My head is a butterfly
Over the traffic jams

Side 33

No jores New Yores
Your whip is so strong
Not all can walk your line
We walk it with our hands
And survive
Like seashell necklaces.

Three Songs From The 50's

Song I

Julito used to shine the soul
of his shoes before he left for
the Palladium to take the wax
off the floor while Tito Rodríguez
flew around the walls like a
parakeet choking Maracas
It was around this time that
Julito threw away his cape
because the Umbrella Man and the
Dragons put the heat on all the
Ricans who used to fly around
in Dracula capes swinging canes
or carrying umbrellas
Even if there was no rain
on the horizon
That same epoca my mother
got the urge to paint the
living room pink and buy a
new mirror with flamingoes
elegantly on the right hand
corner because the one we had
was broken from the time that
Carlos tried to put some respect
Into Julito and knocked the
party out of him.

Song 2

All the old Chevies that the
gringoes from up state New York
wore out
Were sailing around the neighborhood
with dices and San Martín de Porres

el negrito who turned catholic
Hanging in the front windows.

Song 3

There was still no central heating
in the tenements
We thought that the cold was
the oldest thing on the planet earth
We used to think about my Uncle Listo
Who never left his hometown
We'd picture him sitting around
cooling himself with a fan
In that imaginary place
called Puerto Rico.

A Guide to Invention

Once when I was a town a river passed through
my nerves
               Broad and climbing
up a mountain fossils and bones
stuck to my ribs
                    Mi danza mas
approaching total bird's eye view

They had a party in my head
the people tangling with each other
Stories essay ese of the facts
The moon tune of all last night
beginning to chew my hair
Dancing a moon tune in the Square
Dancing the whys
Dancing the hows
If You feel good dance the best moontuny
In all the circles and in all the squares
6 by 8 or 2 by 4
When I was a town and started to blow
up into a city
Buildings like pimples came up through
the floor
Save green mountains in your belly
Make your entry
Into the tubes shining
So si perfect soles overhead
The town goes with the river
to a cave
Darkness
Nothing just like before
anything was created.

The Latest Latin Dance Craze

First
You throw your head back twice
Jump out onto the floor like a
Kangaroo
Circle the floor once
Doing fast scissor works with your
Legs
Next
Dash towards the door
Walking in a double cha cha cha
Open the door and glide down
The stairs like a swan
Hit the street
Run at least ten blocks
Come back in through the same
Door
Doing a mambo-minuet
Being careful that you don't fall
And break your head on that one
You have just completed your first
Step.

Tretis en Dimensional Probability

Poniendo la cosa simply this place that I am going to talk
about is perfect that is within the range of Perfections
whatever those may be to whose ruler or to whatever
understanding you have with God In this place glorious
events are celebrated to the dust of the bone It must be this
way cause that's when you get out Even the flys that come
in the summers the green ones too get in the scope of things
Fall in your eyes buzz by your ears and tell you windows
are open everywhere Everywhere you can get in
everywhere you can get out Through tunnels and pipes by
the doorways All of that adds to the splendor of the roof to
the viewty that from there you get when it is May and your
machine commences to get hot and your mind drifts and
wonders about how did little seeds get inside the maracas or
how they drank the hot chocolate in Switzerland cause that's
what everybody drank when the cold got perverted but an
ear maintains within the music and springs you to see the
river and to see the boats coming in one at a time
                              two at a time
                              three at a time
Now the laws are the laws are the laws are the laws are the
laws but still some have keys that do not fit or open any
door here no where nada Not a Gypsy song for the street
posts Not a Mohican haircut philosofizing through town
scoping the vicinity being swallowed up by the total
center of a cha cha cha
Do not sit still especially if you are within range
of currents the so many fibers and air that construct
From way up top when the moon is landing into the clatter
of dishes and flight of smells it must all look very small
so observing from the towers of creation it was all fabulous
I was created and they were created all form and all space
and all metal that way moving in that direction were created
so the same for the total other direction everything was
everything including many pigeons that flew over our heads
and shit green goo not Gringo On Saturdays wearing
tailored sabored pick-up outfits just out of the cleaners

for 2.10 worth of paper money strollin sometimes this
would occur the reason for this unfortunate situation a
park right around the corner and claro maestro the birds
have to sing and shit (excrement-a word used by people who
know people who don't like shit) but I was never baptized
by their juice It never happened I heard the most minute
sound in the air that was related to an approaching pigeon
and was constantly ducking being where it wasn't raining
Caca or CooCos O simply put like in the beginning bad cosas
                          Manolo Ponce El Fish 3rd Hijo
of his mother great bailarinete of the night club world   It
happened that he was walking once and I was right behind
him and I heard the splashes of the impact and saw his
spontaneous immediate reaction of not knowing what went
down or up what hit him and in what direction for what
where why y más y still más? and then he grabbed his
forehead where he felt it and he felt wet I dropped to the
sidewalk with a laughing attack nobody in the world knows
what was going on The people who were hanging up across
the street all thought that I got shot or something or came
down with something or something came up out of me so
they come running to where I rolled They were breathing
heavy out of air wanting to know Qué pasa So qué pasa
inside the hilariousness I tried to say that that there is
Manolo Ponce he was all dressed up to go to that dance and
the birds got to him By now Manolo was laughing almost
crying cursing bringing down the saints one by one making
them do each the seven deadly sins multiplied and he topped
it off by marching back to his building standing at the top of
the stoop and shouting: I shit on the firecrackers
of the navigators of the assholes of the birds
                          It was all over
his pretty threads and he had to go upstairs and cleanliness
paranoia made him take a bath and re-cologne himself not
re-Colón and go choose another note cause the other played
out Christopher Columbus did know about Colognes and
perfumes It must've been the whiffs of the century coming
from a society which did not bathe much Queen Isabela
jumping in her closet she did not know the mestizos from
East 11th Street in New York or the ones in the Mission of
San Francisco she wanted gold and gold and gold and gold was

used in this part of the world because of its proximity to the rays of the sun and not because you pay hundreds of dollars for it and know nothing of its meaning the sun shining yellow over the mountains and the buildings where now Manolo Ponce has changed and is standing erect in blue and orange attire ready to make his entrance into the world where all the voices and bodies are talking walking quashkinlating minglin in and out of the windows through cement and plastic flowers of all weights and smells and colores he took a step into the world that he knew so well that even at the early age of dance he was aware that anything was possible especially the minute it happens.

The Window

How far from there it is now from that time that you were
sitting around with your friends in that small apartamento
on the Lower East Side and Rafael was talking about spirits
Because his mother and grandmother fabricated their forces
to take meaning shape in his eyes through his mouth talking
at us when all of a sudden the window opened all by it-self
and we said nothing I looked at Chino Chino looked back at
Wilfredo Wilfredo looked straight at Rafael and we looked
at each other and not at the window right quick and we had
to be gently like reawakening because according to us right
there and then our heart physically and psycholy went down
to our asses the window was opened for us to go downstairs
to jump if we wanted to from outside we heard what was out
there we wondered about it all the people at the school that
science teacher could we bring him to see the window what
would he say would he say you guys are crazy insane nothing
like that could happen even if Rafael was telling us that not
all the time can you talk about those those things cause
sometimes they get mad upset cause you don't give them
anything don't spend time with them sharing like Juan
Perez you know what happened to him he didn't want to
believe in nothing so he always needs help to figure
everything out he was told plenty O times what happens the
sun was out going through the Halka that was holding
Rafael's Hairstyle up as he went through the motions telling
us about Juan Perez' biographical highlights that night
Rafael's eyes opened up he went to the toilet and they picked
him up and threw him down repeatedly and Fela was turning
the rice at that precise moment and heard him and she
blames his fear of spirits with destroying the proper
rhythm of her rice which did not fluff that day and what is
rice if it doesn't fluff there has got to be something wrong if
rice does not fluff Juan Perez changed his mind from his
body falling flying like that and began to listen and he left
everything and no one remembers him he went back to a
small pueblo in Puerto Rico where he sits by the road and

reads the cards to strangers who pay him a few quarters or bring him a gardenia for his altar and he says that he prefers this flower to the money it is what they want and you have to always consent to what they want as you put them in their place cause they ain't of this material being they have to be formed into ways to use them don't let them use you only if you in the usage are becoming more like them and what you use is like a part of you like you yourself and he learned from that time that that was his actual fear that was always bugging him knocking on his doors despite him cause he was trying to escape not to notice it Rafael was almost out of air when he finished Wilfredo hairs all over his arms were standing up in a vertical position Chino came out but what about this window it happened so quick the time before it happened a stillness set in total tranquility in the world the people outside the beer cans folding the sound of car tires rolling Good Year's the moment when they caress the tar bumpy down there the ground cement where are the worms on hot and cold New York streets My mother got up one night and said that man is standing outside He is outside right now Rafael was now going deeper She was telling me like that That man is out there now and I know who sent him and I know why they sent him but he will not fulfill his mission he will not bring this home down where they want to see me six feet below the ground Rafael keeps talking he closes his eyes and wrinkles his forehead She took my arm Chino Wilfredo this is real man she took my arm Her hair was down to her waist and it was getting gray and she was moving along in years You will see she said and she pulled me to the door and she opened it slowly and we stuck out our heads and there was this man and he looked O.K. and he said a few things He asked us if the super lived there and if there were any empty apartments in the building cause he and his family had just come in from Mayagüez and needed a place badly my mother Rafael said was looking at the man with a deep mean stare After the man finished talking she started yelling at him no you just go back and don't come back you son of a bitch great whore in Spanish sound more crazy Rafael said it was strange to see how his mother could break out in that tone to a helpless stranger who was looking for

help He too began to search in the man's face and saw the
smile saw the hiddeness of it so his eyes crossed and when
he turned around they both saw that the stranger was at
least four inches off the ground Later that day Rafael and
his mother went to the Botánica on Avenue B and got some
things and went and prepared their door and she made
Ginger tea with cinnamon and milk and put him and his
sister Wanda to sleep early tucking them in bed and
throwing the blankets over their little bodies telling them
that her grandfather was not afraid of anything in his day
and he knew about the spirits where they hung out and how
they came and went and when where why and that he was
always there with them taking care of them and that if they
occasioned to see him in their lives not to run or be scared
but that to see it as blessing to see that he was telling them
something that they should be alert right then this big roach
fell from the ceiling into the center of things and Chino was
going to assassinate it but we cooled him down cause them
roaches can talk to you about the millennium and they know
Polish jokes and eat bagels and read the Kabala and they
eliminate you trying to eliminate them The only thing is
that you never eat one thinking that it is a red kidney bean
"beans mark of the devil" as the old folks go when they
mention the red beans so popular with onions and pumpkin
and tomato sauce and pig's feet apparently Chino once ate a
roach that was involved with some beans and every time he
sees one (roach or bean) he remembers Rafael just looked
at him and said you're still alive ain't you what doesn't kill
gets you fat we all broke out laughing rollin receiving
breeze sereno from the opened window which made a whole
in our memories.

Frutilandia

Spurts in the memory you see your tongue all her tongues
hanging out loosely like the final solo of the guitar
All the things you would not have said Peel another orange
while you wait for results She had a face like an avocado
She had a face like a mango Her brother who was not there
had a face that looked like an orange Her face was just like
that like an apple Her face was like the inside of the
tamarindo She had a face that looked like a pear A man who
was there had a face that looked like a wrench or a bar
not where you drink like he was but a bar Not far from
where the musical piano formulated a theory of Calculus
arriving up into poetry that one night she was there and she
had a face that looked like the interior of a guava before it is
opened A friend of hers was there with a face like a
tangerine later you could detect the fragrance of tangerine
on her blouse Her face looked like the first full moon being
looked at from some freshwater creek running atop a
mountain There was a fellow there and his face looked like a
thousand disciplined bananas She did not dance with the guy
who had a wrench face Why did she behave this way But
she did dance with the guy with the tangerine face There
was someone there that had eyes that looked like great juicy
concord grapes staring at you penetrating making you
wonder about things Some two or three persons had faces
that looked oval like perfect potatoes She had a round
mysterious peach face The tangerine was in the peaches and
the avocado in the orange Or was it the apple next to the
guava in arrangement there was so many people there
raining in the back and the front was dancing her tongue on
the wall philosophically speaking only Did they see it as a
bottle or a battle Who left? Who came ?
          Who   ? Where   What   ? and finally ?
          Her face looked like something from a planet where
the sun never goes down Never goes down the sun and one
toke will sustain you through ropes of reality on Avenue A,
B, C, D in Minor Through farmlands and chilly Wisconsin
and crazy Detroits Blowing Okie tops in Oregon Geee Be
woooofs what you Mama got in her belly inside the earth

deep mushroom juice staircase He and she were by the wall
and they began to look like a guanávana like two big
guanávanas floating like the Good Year blimp announcing in
colors over the San Francisco heads Conserve yourself in
the rhythm when it gets steady whipping and hold on to the
rope of the horse that you fly Steady pounding eternal
insistence the clave bouncing stripping the moments

                            In short grasps the
imagination chops up memory and nothing is recalled right
and all gets blurry in the darkness you don't know where
nothing is O es anything all those things you presume You
thought you left it all there standing still So difficult to
focus with the shades of nightclub walls rumba walls
silhouettes Cafe drink Rum And Koke Brandy Sniffer
Whiskey Chaser Bloody Mary y pronto viene el Crazy Harry
Brandy Alexander El Gran Domecque But he approached the
bar and said Martell without the ice His teeth told others
that he knew what he was talking about the way he hanged
them inside his mouth But he came to the bar and told the
bartender Un Martell minus hielo But it came to the bar
and asked for a 7 High Her lips part gently and her tongue
slow drags cha cha out The song from the bands starts up
and they singing:
                    "that tongue that you have will be your
                        ruin"
All you can do is wander into town all you can do is wonder
into the city all you can do is wonder swallow the drawings
being created by the dancers in on through the air with
their bodies waving like a blanket getting smoke under its
legs like the ocean looks from far away circular chewing
machine where you could clear your wounds and leave your
depressions outside as you make a run for it Her name was
in the interior of the question involved She flickered like a
match when she threw away the ball not the balls a certain
beyond the lines of excellence her presence mugging the
oxygen molecules on to the sheets of smallest air she touch
his head inside the 5 of clubs smoothly the crowds
transform deform shake up and split act nervous go home
get home turn on the light and look around for what smells
good go into the room where you sleep the light sees you go
on and shuts itself off

By Lingual Wholes

1980-1982

Borinkins in Hawaii

For Norma Carr, Blaise Sosa
And Ayala and his famous corner

In 1900
A ship left San Juan Harbor
Full of migrant workers
Of the fields
En route to what they believed
To be California
Instead something like C&H
Which managed the vessel
With strings like a puppet
From afar
Took them to Hawaii

When Toño who was one of them
And Jaime who was another
And Felipe who was a third
Of the many 8,000 who took
This spin
Saw Hawaii they thought they
Were still in Puerto Rico
It took movement of time
Show up of the wind
It took the Japanese currents
To convince them
That in somewhere they were

Sugar was the daddy on the
Commecial horizon
Donuts for everybody
Ah history was getting sweet
If you wasn't a cane worker
With sores on your feet
And corns on your hands
Under the sun for how much
A day

Sugar was gonna blow flesh up
Sugar mania
Sugar come from cane
Get some cane
Get some workers
Get some land

The United States talked to the
Old Hawaiian queen
It was a polite conversation
The gringo merely pointed
To where the Marines
Were casually placed
Just that
The Hawaiian Kingdom
Pieces of Cake
Littered on the Pacific

"What in the mountain got
Into you Toño to wanna come
From where you were
To jump on this boat
To come to this other planet
Look a volcano to lite your
Cigar, a desert for your
Camel, what is this the
End of the world, HA."

"Well Jaime look a guava
And coconut is coconut
See that tree where a Pana
Hangs. Smell the flowers
Fragrance like Aguas Buenas."
Thru each Pana-pen a metropolis
Of juices and texture
Ulus are Pana-pens in Puerto Rico
Ulus:Hawaii
Pana-pen: Puerto Rico
Breadfruit for you
Ulus hang like earrings
From the ears of women

On the tree
A blue dress on top
The curve is the horizon
A reminder that we all live
On a Pana-Pen

Hawaii fuedal 19th century
Catholic liturgy
Thru the flower tops
The best years of
Tomás-Toñón
Jaime
Felipe and the full migration
Living in camps
Box homes for workers
And their families
Early risers
church on Sunday
Machete on Monday
Orange curtains thru
The greenery
Cuatro strings
With the bird speech
The pick pickers of
Pineapple stress the
Décima
As back in Borinkin
Ya se men
In ten lines you hem
A skirt
In Kohala they call it
Cachy-cachy
People jumpy-jumpy
Like roosters
The cuatro guitar chirps
Squeeky its note in the
Upper C high nose pitch
Sound of the Arawak
Garganta of the Areyto
Song gallery of the
Ancient inhabitants

Of the boat Borinkin

Broken guitars navigating
Vessles
Arrive like seed onto the
Ground
Whatever is in the dirt
Will come out
We're gonna finger pop
The pineapple
The cane is gonna fly
The mayordomos will whip
Ankles
Secret hidden wood
Will get them
There are dark passages of night
Roads under the kona trees
In the dark the sound kaploosh
On the skull
The mayordomos are paid
By the plantation owners
The wood is made by nature

At Ayalas Place
3rd & 4rth generation Puerto Ricans
Hawaiians
Eat rice and beans prepared
By Japanese woman
Soya sauce on the tables
Hawaii only Puerto Rican
Oriental community in the
World

A ship which left San Juan
Turn of the century
Transported workers music
And song
They thought they were
California bound
But were hijacked by
Corporate agriculture

Once they got to land
They folded over
They grew and mixed
Like Hawaii can mix
Portuguese sausage slit
Inside banana leaf
Filipino Japanese eyes
Stare from mulatto faces

The Portuguese brought
The ukulele to anxious fingers
Who looked at the motion of
Palm leaves to help them search
For a sound
They studied the designs of
The Hula dancers
And made
A guitar which sounds like
It's being played by the
Fingers of the breeze

They all dance cachy-cachy
And jumpy-jumpy
In places like Hilo
And Kohala
You hear the shouts
You hear the groans
You feel the wind of the
Cane workers' machete
And in the eyes you see
The waves of the oceans
You see beads
Which form a necklace
Of islands
Which have emerged out of
The tears.

Anonymous

And if you lived in those olden times
With a funny name like Choicer or
Henry Howard, Earl of Surrey, what chimes!
I would spend my time in search of rhymes
Make sure the measurement termination surprise
In the court of kings snapping till woo sunrise
Plus always be using the words *alas* and *hath*
And not even knowing that that was my path
Just think on the Lower East Side of Manhattan
It would have been like living in satin
Alas! The projects hath not covered the river
Thou see-est vision to make thee quiver
Hath I been delivered to that "wildernesse"
So past
I would have been the last one in the
Dance to go
Taking note the minute so slow
All admire my taste
Within thou *mambo* of much more haste.

The Physics of Ochun

A group of professional
scientists
from Columbia University
heard that in an old
tenement apartment
occupied by a family
named González
a plaster-of-Paris
statue made in Rome
of Caridad del Cobre
started crying
The scientists
curious as they are
took a ride across
town to investigate
After stating their purpose
and their amazement
they were led to the
room where the statue was
Sure enough it was wet
under the eyes
Overnight, Señora González
told them, it had cried so
much that they were able
to collect a jar full of tears
The scientist almost knocked his
gold-rim glasses off his face
May we have this as a specimen
to study in our laboratory?
She agreed, and they took a taxi
with the jar to Columbia
They went directly to the lab
to put the tears through a
series of tests
They put a good amount of
the liquid under their
Strongest Microscope

Lo and behold!
What they saw made them loosen
their neckties
There inside the liquid
clearly made out through
the microscope was the
word: JEHOVAH
No matter how much they
moved the water they
kept getting the word
They sent for a bottle of
scotch
They served themselves in test tubes
They called the González family
to see if they could explain
All the González family knew
was that it was the tears
of Caridad del Cobre
They explained to Señora González
what was happening
She said that weirder than that
was the fact that her
window had grown a staricase
that went up beyond the clouds
She said she and her daughter
had gone up there to check it
out
because, she told them, a
long white rope had come out
of their belly buttons and some-
thing was pulling them up
What happened? the enthusiastic
scientists from Columbia University
wanted to know
We went up there and were
massaged by the wind
We got hair permanents
and our nails manicured
looking a purple red
My daughter says she saw
a woodpecker designing the

air
The scientists put the phone down
and their eyes orbited the room
We have to get out there
Incredible things are happening
They rushed back out
and into the González residency
they entered
It's in the same
room with the statue
They rushed in and went to the
window
So amazed were they
they lost their speech
All their organs migrated an inch
Clearly in front of them
a 3-foot-wide marble stair
which went up into the sky
The scientists gathered themselves
to the point of verbalizing again
They each wanted to make sure
that the other was "cognizant"
of the *espectáculo*
Once they settled upon reality
they decided that the urge to
explore was stronger than their
fears
One decided to take a writing pad
to take notes
One decided to take a test tube
in case he ran into substances
One decided to take a thermometer
and an air bag to collect atmosphere
Señora González, would you please
come up with us?
They wanted to know if she would
lead them up
if you could see it you could touch
it, she told them
She went out first and they
followed

The marble steps were cold
They could have been teeth of
the moon
As they went up the breeze smiled
against their ears
The murmur of the streets dimmed
They were climbing and climbing
when they felt a whirlpool in
the air
For sure it was the hairdresser
Señora González sensed the odor of
many flowers in the breeze
The scientist with the test tube
saw it get full of a white liquid
The scientist with the air bag
felt it change into a chunk of metal
The scientist with the writing pad
saw a language appear on it backwards
printing faster than a computer
the paper got hot like a piece of
burning wood
and he dropped it down into the
buildings
It went through an open widow
and fell into a pot of red beans
A woman by the name of Concepción was
cooking
Frightened she took it to a doctor's
appointment she had the next day
She showed it to the physician
who examined it
He thought it was the imprint
of flower petals
so even and bold in lilac
ink
The dream Concepción had during
the night came back to her
I know what's going on, doctor
I'll see you in nine months
Walking she remembered forgetting

to put the *calabaza* into the beans
and rushed home sparkling in
her yellow dress

Two Guitars

Two guitars were left in a room all alone
They sat on different corners of the parlor
In this solitude they started talking to each other
My strings are tight and full of tears
The man who plays me has no heart
I have seen it leave out of his mouth
I have seen it melt out of his eyes
It dives into the pores of the earth
When they squeeze me tight I bring
Down the angels who live off the chorus
The trios singing loosen organs
With melodious screwdrivers
Sentiment comes off the hinges
Because a song is a mountain put into
Words and landscape is the feeling that
Enters something so big in the harmony
We are always in danger of blowing up
With passion
The other guitar:
In 1944 New York
When theTrío Los Panchos started
With Mexican & Puerto Rican birds
I am the one that one of them held
Tight   like a woman
Their throats gardenia gardens
An airport for dreams
I've been in theatres in *cabarets*
I played in an apartment on 102nd street
After a baptism pregnant with women
The men flirted and were offered
Chicken soup
Echoes came out of hallways as if from caves
Someone is opening the door now
The two guitars hushed and there was a
Resonance in the air like what is left by
The last chord of a *bolero*

The Process of Bolero

Pushing a big heart through a small
pen is not difficult
Through a six-string guitar
the heart comes out red first
It is followed by the rest
of the organs
In the love song tradition
which says it is better
For the one that leaves
than for the one who stays
One follows a sigh
The other swims in tears
Your heart is an oven
and a generation puts their
Cookies in it
They say the furnace has
its windows in the eyes
In the songs of love
the heart comes through the
mouth
It is followed by the whole
body
Your soul jumps next through
your throat
making holes in the air
        burning up pages

Ironing Goatskin

The air is suffocating
In the altar which is the sky
The sun the only statue
On this beach the vibrations
Of the drums
The fat barrels of the Bomba
The Papa, the Mama, and the Niño
The way the sound goes up
Your head goes seaward on *canucas*
Listen
Mercy for the goat flesh, please
The drummers look at the
Mahogany legs of the girls
Who enter the round Bomba circle
And proceed to imitate them
Turning the visual into sound
There isn't a place to sit your
Lungs down
It is for this reason
That we should be concerned
with the destiny of goats.

Here
Is an Ear
Hear

Is the ocean really inside seashells
or is it all in your mind?—Pichón de la Once

Behold and soak like a sponge.
I have discovered that the island of Puerto Rico
is the ears of Saru-Saru, a poet reputed to have lived
in Atlantis. On the day that the water kissed and
embraced and filled all the holes of that giant
missing link, this bard's curiosity was the greatest
for he kept swimming and listening for causes.
He picked up rocks before they sank and blew
wind viciously into them. Finally he blew so hard
into a rock that he busted his ear drums; angry,
he recited poems as he tried turning into a bird
to fly to green Brazil. His left ear opened up
like a canal and a rock lodged in it. Rock attracts
rock and many rocks attached to this rock. It got
like a rocket. His ear stayed with it in a horizontal
position. Finally after so many generations he got
to hear what he most wanted: the sounds made by flowers
as they stretched into the light. Behold, I have
discovered that the island of Puerto Rico is the
ears of Saru-Saru.

Prescriptions
from the plantnet

*When they prepare to find the answer to what has been asked
them, they eat an herb called cohoba, either ground or ready
to be ground, and they inhale the smoke of it through their
nostrils, and this makes them go out of their minds and see
visions. When the power and properties of the herb have
worn off, they regain their senses. They tell what they have
seen and heard in their council with the gods, and say that
God's will will be done.*

—Francisco López de Gómara, *Historia General de las Indias*

The Mint Family—*Yerba buena*

If your stomach starts to come to your brain, go hunting for
this scent. From the pores outside your nervous system will
come stage lights. Makes your bowels like a Pacific ship.
You'll hear the stems converted to flutes. The nigh wraps
you in a blue haze.

Albaca

To go toward a cow by a river where women sit by the edges
banging clothes on rocks, only you will not see any of this for
you are the fish.

Pasote

One step at a time you enter the veins of the leaf, you enter a
slide where your feet are worth nothing. Down this funnel
you are going like water in a tube. The passage puts you on
the other side of flesh or an eyeball coming out of a cliff.

Patchouli

At the bottom of an old Spanish trunk I found patchouli
because the odor preserves the thread that must survive
through time. Perfume for your closets or tropical
mothballs.

Mejorana

Mejor que Ana, Nada.

Anamú

Depending on which part of the branch you pick up, one side
has a monster called Umanasata; the other has a princess, La
Ana of Mu. Oh, the art of bending down.

Rompe Saraqüey

Entrevu into that head; what you realize is that you didn't
need it. It also breaks Saras crab.

Yerba Bruja

Take your nose off, take your ears off, take your eyes out,
unscrew you skull, place it in a pot and boil; she will come
in a beautiful green robe and drink you but she will throw
out the juice witch is which.

Ruta

If you get stuck on the route, call Rota-Ruta to flush you out;
then you see clearly a pipe with seven keys and a tribe of
feathers behind you.

Yerba Luisa

A girl named Luisa sits on the grass. To meet her you'd have to take a bath. Down your back she will slide. When you come out you will never see grass again, and Luisa will have nowhere to sit. This is the beginning of imagination.

Sofrocotón

Comes from the blue trees abundant on Jajuya road leading into Good Waters. Fry this leaf with eucaliptino twigs and rub on any pain, but never eat the fruits of this tree, for they are too high to reach, and if they fall they are too ripe to eat.

Almistris

Take down from branch with left hand on first Wednesday of any month; otherwise, it will work in reverse. It will make you see the color blue as green: the sky would look like an avocado and you like a mouth that's eating the truth.

Alta Misa

A mass celebrated in a land higher than the Andes. Your organs will have sensations of being vertical in heaven's line while your skeleton sits in a nightclub where the juke box was invented.

Borete

Great for eliminating stains like those caused by green bananas.

Salvia

If your molar was extracted by the town nut impersonating a dentist, place this leaf on the space and the bleeding will stop, like turning an industrial switch.

Malva

Boil it with cloth rags. Put those rags over any pain. Before it leaves it shellacs the bones. Your flesh feels like it's pressed against ball bearings. Next time you ache, take Malva.

Satosoti

Weird, because after you pull it off the branch it keeps jumping like a jumping bean. Sometimes you got to hit it with something; any object of good weight will do. When it gets down to its thing it has no comparison; it is an anti-dizziness drug.

Tobacco

Anesthesia. Immediate delivery to any wound of the flesh to halt its bleeding. Smoke to blow away earaches. Nicotinia to rid your house of mosquitos. Cable for the phone calls of the mediums.

Lemon Tree Leaves and Flor Tilo

If your nerves have gone haywire from too much thinking of ideal situations that never materialize, drink some tea out of this plant and you settle down almost into a nod. The world could blow up but you tranquil.

Guarapo de Maguey

Tired of your blood? Send a broom down with it. Sweep up all the bad particles. You'll be like a whistle. A drink of this could have saved Ponce de León instead of giving him that run around.

Flor de Roble

Goodbye, Dr. Scholls. You put this leaf on your corns and pop corns.

Mala Madre

In Shakespearean it is known as spider plant. You take the leaves and dry them. Later boil the tea out of them. If you have any grease this will be for you; grease will dissolve like addicts at the arrival of narcos.

Fideillo

So fierce that as it grows out of the ground it chokes neighboring plants. It doesn't care; it could be a sweet rose. Some things out here can also kill; that's why you can't be so happy-go-lucky. Something can crawl up your leg and choke you. It could be your last botanical kick.

Bacalao and Society

Cod fish thinks underwater
The Portuguese tend to go after it
In the form of dry cod it was the
food of the exploration voyages
Surrounded by salt the first currency
it stayed ready each day more salty
But once in the pot hot water can
debate it and portions of it leave
Everything 'cept milk can be put
into it
Swift net Portugales
on the dish
on the coast
live on wood atop the liquid
after the cod salt
Flamboyante Catholic dances
Roman apparel for the building
For wedding or baptism
fry cod or boil it
onions or tomato sauce
the height of tears
The whole palette a furnace
where *bacalao* melts
The whole street an orange dream
Where she walks
and where for she he walks
The lowered house white on blue
heaven
The smell of *bacalao a la vizcaína*
makes your head also turn
Eyes push open a curtain
Music escapes every time a salt
pebble divides in half
For cooking long hours you need time
and songs which hum within you
your finger tips are mouths
so stubborn when it goes into the

hot water
It comes out shaky and loose
spreading apart into layers
The finger is warm from hot water
and clean from lemon
The thumb should press what you
consider to be the head of each
piece
It breaks in half with edges of
fiber
Your relation to a sea
or a mountain determines what
you put around it
The Portuguese got all parts of
the world
Outside a million things
inside one word for it
They divide tribes for domination
Like a big octopus whose arms did
reverse after touching fire
It went back into itself
They go fishing like looking for gods
Back home to sun falling wine
In Bahia, Rio Piedras, Camaqüey to rum
the favorite and most coquette
Tune is Bacalao a la serenade.

Art This

Lucy Comancho is an artist
Art this
She makes all the stars in Hollywould
seem like flashlights which have
been left turned on for a week
She had a *frenesí*
A friend in C
A friendinme
with paintings and blowing things
up into color which came from nowhere
No one knows where she got these things
Her mother says too much thinking
She painted the walls in her house
She painted the hallways and stairs
the stoops the garbage can tops the
squares in the sidewalk the tar on the
street the plastic bags from the cleaners
the brown grocery bags the inside of milk
containers She herself had to be contained
from painting your face the closest layer
of the sky elements everything she gave
brush to rush to paint your *nalgas* if you
gave her room She never thought of canvas
where they sell it absent from her view
Sometimes she was called Picassa feminizing
Picasso
She painted Josefina as I was writing
that Josefina is the feminine of José
Josés who are also known to go under the
nicknames of Cheos or Pepes and so
Josefina got tagged on her the name Pepa
which is female for Pepe and she dug that
Pepa for if you look close the other name
José y *fina* means José and thin or sounds
like *oficina* like Joseoffice also it had
something in it of José is *fina* José is
finis finished no this for someone being

composed by an artis
To top it off Pepa also means *pit*
you see what is inside of fruits This
is all in Spanish and something is being
lost in the translation just like you lose
your natural color when you leave a tropical
country and come to a city where the sun
feels like it's constipated Ask Lucy Comancho
She knows about all this
art this
artis.

Cinco de maya

The Greek Theater
in Berkeley
Gets full like a
Bowl
Corn-maidens
Barley princesses
Ryo toast
Wave their spring
Bushies
At Zeus-Apollo
As the singers are
Them
What's come to be
From the mouth
The meter
DEMETER
Pluto's rope
Lassoes at the
Various *personificadas*

The eyes are gloves
Baseball flowers

La Voice filters
Shango sprayers
The air
Plumed serpent
Circles this
Egg-shaped zero
Springs all
Motherflethers

Amphitheater
Musically 3 beats
2 beats clave lawyer
Oval *pelota* going
Toward everybodie's

Top head Sun
Hang on to your
Round *platos*

Dance and touch
The hands
Of distance
Sweet *contemplato*
From afar
Syrup in the
Fruit bowl
Inside

Plato knew the
Sun was here
This gorgeous
Theater
Of his people

THEOS-CALLI

Geography of the
Trinity Corona

Galicia Gypsy tongue sucks salt water
Red fish *gitana* de Galicia
Sings
Romany *de* Hindus
Romany *de* Hindus
Ibericos boats from the soul
Boats from Ibericos lust
Schizophrenic ships search golden dust
Ladinos
Ladinos
Ancient Spanish
Ancient Spanish
Lengua del Kabala
Kabala *lengua*
O Mohamet *flor del este*
Flor este del Mohamet
Sonrisa of same people
Flor de maya
Lengua primordial agua y sal
Mora eyes of paradise
Gypsy Freeway
Gypsy Freeway
Mohamet
Ladinos
Romany *de* Hindus
Valencia
Where sound parked in the tongue
Galicia *con pan*
Pan Galicia
Pan pan Ibericos
Bridge made of white handkerchiefs
To the cascabells of Andalusia
Walking light on the loose
Gone through the strings of sitars
Guitars / Sitars

My strings are here
A sí
Cadiz *cámara* my friends
In the pupils of time
Jump barefoot into the circle dance
Here come the Romanies
Islamicals
The Rock of Gibraltar
Rock of Tarik
Like the wave of the ocean
After retreat

On the sand it leaves pearls
From the bottom
Shaped like three-dimensional mandalas

Take my boat
Take my boat

Gallegos *gitanos*
Jump the Arawaks
The *michicas*
Who had gold like we have the air
Golden halos
Of Maya Cocos
Taínos skidding through
Carib sea on canoes
Church pierced the mountain
Gallelocos everywhere
Cement came down from heaven
Taíno areyto echoes from the flora
Gone through the pipe of time
Into the face
Into the cheek so cute
España danza
Africoco bembé
Burundanga mixture is the word
Bembé Mohamet *Areyto*
Layered peacock cake
Sandwhich of language

Take my boat
Take my boat

Yoruba y Arare
Lucumi
Cascabels of Romany gypsies
Nativo antillano
Hindus
Gallegos
Africano
Caribe
Rythmic circle
The islands are beads
of a necklace
Tarot cards with tobacco smoke
Crescent moon
The handshake of Fatima
Golden and red hot rubies
Chains where sacraments hang
Symphony of
Moorish flamenco
Fans opening like sound
Out of the acoustic mama bass
Streets of Islam wrapped in
Catholic robes
Where they say an eye for an eye
Teeth for teeth
Jump for jump
Make my Spanish lamp
Make my Spanish lamp
Walk the camels into the gardens
Electric flowers
See them shine
Make my Indian time
Make my Indian time
Song is memory
Memory is song
Take my boat
Take my boat
Make my African Alphabet
Skin on skin

Mohamet Africanos
Look the street is full of
Ethiopians
Look Jersey City full of
Taínos
Gitanos *lindos*
Lucumi inside Yucaye
White angels come from
Arare drums
Visual spectacle envied
by rainbow
Look Pakistani mambo
The ears are the musical race
Even polish my Polish
Mazurka in the *guava* villages
Blood vessels of combined chemistry
From everywhere to someone
Galicia
Romany *de* Hindus
Arawaki
Arare
Moro
Lucumi
Iberios
Mohammedans
Gypsy
Yoruba
Taínos
Colors turn into sounds
We start building cities
From blueprints
Found in the sails
Of remember

Take my boat
Take my boat

The Low Riders

Who first in the human planet invented the wheel, its use as
transport, now see it someone caressing a mountain
watching rocks and pebbles rolling, coming to a stop in
front of their toes, just picture, gee, if we were ants
clinging, or something more minute unnamed creatures of
the tropical berserk, an orange pin head moving with eight
legs, the ancients must have said how quickly this carries it
through the terrain. Now the first hatch back would have
been inside rocks, or in the dream to be a pelota
flying through a Taíno park, send a message which travels
distance and I can catch it with my fingers.
    Out here puffing, jamming, moving down boulevard,
deep into the industry of tires, red wheels, blue tires,
metal sunk low around it, like a closed eye or a blink,
constructions floating, home made interiors, Roman
Chariots dodging, truncks full of batteries. In Peru the
llama was freight carrier over through mountains paths
whose history they were starting, for gasoline they gave
them Chicha and coca leaves, zoom through streams, atop
where it's cold down to the hot flatlands, edges of towns
where they traded woven blankets and disappeared into the
clouds. And that petro took them through sky tree branches,
the llama white and bushy, serene, a caravan of miniature
camels.
    When I am in this room that flies it is as if I invented
rubber. Like San Jose Low riders interiors, fluffy sit
back, unwind, tattoo on left hand, near the big thumb a
cross with four sticks flying, emphasizing its radiance,
further up the arm skeletons, fat blue lines, Huichol
designs on the copper flesh, the arm of the daddy-o
on the automatic stick. A beautiful metal box which many
call home. It doesn't matter if the manufacturer was Ford
or General Motors, their executives in the suburbs of
Detroit watching home movies, vacationing in weird
Londons, when the metal is yours you put your mark on it,
buying something is only the first step, what you do to it is
your name, your history of angles, your exag-

geration, your mad paint for the grand scope of humanity, the urbanites will see them like butterflies with transmissions. Take it to Mexico and get a round figure to the maniacs of Tijuana, who break it down to slices, throw it back together, slice it up again.

Once a circus caravan of riders from Watsonville took twenty cars down, puffing and flying and bouncing all the way; only stopped twice by Highway Patrol, but they looked so looney, that the officers perhaps behind a beer or two, let them go, saying this can't be real, plus they were clean as a Mormon in Salt Lake City, license and registrations, and hydraulics well hidden.

Zoom, all enroute toward TJ to get their interiors layed out, they know who to see, one tall Tony, another guy called Gordo, talk right adjust your price, Tigar, Zebra, velvet, polka dots, colors your dream, shit never heard of, tugged in tight, last you a century, you go before your call will, blazing stuff shag rug pink running across dashboard.

Twenty cars rolling, eating the road from here to Tijuana, from here to Tía Juana, music from the Pioneers. All the mozos some with mozas sporting lumberjack shirts, leaning, brown hands, the tattoo cross where Christ was tortured, on the streering wheel cutting edges, a mosaic of tongues rattling, can we say unidentified flying objects, private discos, patterns, a piece here and a piece there, if that don't work enter the garage of spare parts.

Mission Street is El Camino Real, is the old road of Christianity, if you start riding from 24th you could go in a straight line all the way to the gates of gold. From path to road from road to street to avenue from avenue to boulevard from boulevard to airport from airport continue to space station, looking for those white crystals, don't kid yourself the Northern proposition has always been vertical, an uptown kind of motion, towards the mechanics who lay out your interior, how real is the Camino, El Camino Irreal where car junkies glide into the southern and northern lights.

The scene on the road must be here comes Ali-baba and his twenty machines, going South to get to their North. But wait, how long will this oil supply last. 2050, you cannot replace it like coffee or tobacco, Columbian oil gives its own

seeds, but the blood of the earth once it's taken out leaves
space. Do you figure they will be able to equip motors with
new gadgets that will allow them to digest an alternate source
of energy, *si no, se acabó la Honda*. The whole landscape
will be full of rust, only the low riders pleasure boats will
be assigned to museums. Tony blows: And my hand against
that dashboard, in my studio roving, dazzling right below
the mini charro hat swinging from the rear view mirror,
with its embroidery in gold and silver, gold rings you bunch
of susus, exhibit relaxation, the State of California
made the roads for us, the princesses in shiny cabins.

Who invented wheels, invented roads, but movement
which is before avenues, before circles invented itself, it
made enough of itself to be available to all, to be interpreted
according to each, its like you enter and perform, like the
full fleet of twenty cars riding towards TJ will each have its
own coat, their common language is their closeness to the
ground, they want to kiss the earth, they want to penetrate
the many disguises of their mama land, have we been in
touch with you are we rubbing you right, to be on this
road is this the way we say love dangling from a window
driving Smokey Robinson and the Miracles, OoooooBaby,
Baby OoooooBabyBaby, green light go, stop light red stop,
yellow light put your feet down tight, in the hot rod land
what can we do with our hands but attack the street, mold it,
make it unique, each will be different for the same purpose.

Hector blows: When my cacharro goes down there's not
even room to stick a nickle in at the bottom. The steering
wheel is the handle of measurement, skinny ones, made of
silver chains, prisoner chains, industrial chains, smoking
chains, the smaller steering wheels allow for quick jerky
precise turns, tricks that only road runner could perform,
beep beep, make room for the modern car yachts of the
Watsonville Road Kings, monarchs of the boulevards, never
bored always going somewhere, now enroute south, towards
the land of the articulate mechanics, who work with their
eyes closed and create short of putting a toilet in the back. A
style of craftsmanship, concentration, it features remnants
of a classical point of view, the car is the living room, like
Gothic mixed with Toltecas, my space to freak you out, come
delight in my red peach fuzz sofas, enjoy the stereo sound

from my Pioneer speakers, picture the chromo hanging like
a painting in a gallery, car club emblems showing through
the back windows: Watsonville Road Kings, jumping and
moving, cleaning the surface, when the gasoline stops
pumping the vehicles will run on perfume and music.

ISLANDIS:

The Age of Seashells

Puerto Rico & California
1984-1987

Hot Thought

The idea that something called
the Green House effect is at
hand
Enhances when you perceive it from
the Caribbean
From Caguas for instance
or deeper yet Coamo
Where between 12 noon and
3
Even ice in the freezer
loses its stance
Is it gonna get hotter than
this?
Will we reach the point where
our flesh tenderizes
Slowly cooks and fills the
air with an aroma of perhaps
fried fish or pork
And will we then see our
skin slide off our bones
and drop onto the street
As we walk across the plaza
making a last attempt to get to
the coconut ice cream vender
before they both melt.

Estudios Mentales
Sub-titulado:
Los locos tienen sueños normales

Shhhheeeeeee. La verdad es que tu mente está en tus pies
te han estao metiendo embuste Malabé Piensa de abajo pa
riba y tú vas a ver Quién le metería en los seso a esta
gente que el órgano de pensar está en el cráneo Si hasta
los títeres saben correr y el profesor encerrao
con esos libros y cuando se va amarral los zapatos hay
que llamar una ambulancia Algunos de estos libros tienen
retratos de los sesos Un enredo de Esphagetti gordo y
estos dibujos para tratar de convencerte de que tu mente
está en tu cabeza Pero yo sé que la mente es lo que
anda y lo que corre Perdónenme yo sé que son muchas las
desilusiones pero soporten esta nueva información con
calma anden despacio por el espacio Aguántate Nicasio
cógelo suave No ves que el universo es un baile divino
Pregúntate qué es lo más que baila en el planeta casino.

Islandis

Could the apples of Hesperiedes
been the guavas on Cheos
Property
That converted into the sweetest
eyes
That could be borrowed from the
sun
Could these Carib isles
been in Platos plume
In the philosophers mind
a garden of amapolas
Stretching from the red soil
Towards the lamps of the
Gods
Mayaqüez plain Maya
before the Castillian Quez
Where else is Quez from
Where else Is Maya from
Was the town of my birth
a stepping stone towards
Atlantis
In dreams of boats canucas
parked off Humacao
Gold and red coral
Songs of guiding nymphs
Tunneling out of spiral
shells
Could Coquis have been the
singing notes that
Drove Homers sailors mad
into the sea
Atlantits as big as
Guanábanas
In barrio square
Hanging on a Carmenet
Like a hidden fountain
in Cordova

Let us bow our heads
in silence
Pushed back to the twilight
of ideas
And with the next Venusian
light to telegram into
Manatí
Declare ourselves
the kings and queens
of Posiedon
Wearing crowns of
verdant feathers.

La simplicidad de la imagen

Tu cabeza llena
La cama vacía.

Don Arturo says:

When I was young
there was no difference
Between the way I danced
and the way tomatoes
Converted themselves
into sauce
I did the waltz or a
guaguanco
Which ever one your rhythm
which ever one your song
The whole town was caressed
to sleep with my two-tone
Shoes
Everyone
had to leave me alone
On the dirt or on the wood
they used to come from far
and near
Just to say look at Arturo
disappear.

Invisibility O

Planets of air
angels and music
between us all
Humidity penetrated
by a screw of molecules
Global bubbles
pink and hazy
Glass teeth without
bodies
Invisible gobs of manure
synchronized with space
Waves
Transparent porky-dogs
Monsters created by
ant-eaters fucking mountain
Swine in thought
A worm the size of
a ship moving
Between the cities
Dressed in ultraviolet fog
Insane moans moving
thru hallway of clouds
Where fly holy spirit birds
who eat electric umbilical
wires
Which are plugged into the
hole in your soul
Melting into vagabundo spirits
vacationing in matter
Chunks of atmosphere
between us
Folks is full of monstrous
images
which make horror flicks seem
polite
Earth contaminated
by objects of unknown dimensions

With breaths of sulfuric gasses
Passages of murky soup
like hippopotamus saliva
Mixed with bull's brain
and school yard basketball
Players sweat
Mist of carbon dioxide
on wings of bats with
Vampires lust
The discussion minerals are
having made visible in three
Dimensions
Lead transmitting rays to copper
Copper smoking into silver
Silver music begging the ears
of gold
Talking about alchemy
The man who ate a dollar bill
and shitted four quarters
Sheet of memory traveling
endless planks of atoms
Juices of emotion making
lightning sounds from mars
Luciferian radiation beaming
down from Venus
Primeval spaces where tobacco
was a theory
A telephone call from Caquax
Mountains whose dress is a
gown of blue cystals called sky
Orchestra of reptilian musicians
blowing into caves like trumpets
Echoes make the heavens
shingaling
Ears floating without flesh
like helium baloons
Fall into dance position
Making an oval like the
island of Puerto Rico
Moose and bull horns
are antennas for cable

Thoughts of red frangrance
Dreams of Andalusian pirates
masterbating into Atlantic Ocean
After seelng Cordova mermalds
pop out the water in their heads
Vengeful skeletons jumping out
of air pockets
Collecting cemetery prayers
and candle fumes
Between us is doors made of the
aroma of dead flowers
Azucenas and condiamores
the campana of hallucinogenic flight
a firm of words which are pictures
over the florida trees red sparks
Shooting from Jagüeyes barrio
In mountain so high
Nectar left by butterflies
in their tranquil flight
Bees hear bells blasting
out of black coffee cups and orbit
like spuntniks around the earth
the sky looks like a page
full of clouds
above the cross of the Catholic
church

Over Aguas Buenas the Virgin of
Monserrate jumps rope from stars
to moon
With her blue cape
She empties out into the irises
of sleeping girls
Who wake up open their windows
and with their moorish eyes
Put the flowers to sleep

Between us is a lake of humidity
Where sound is like light bulbs
Space cadets shift into memory
Memory makes a horn of air

Where your desires sparkle
and beg eternity for love.

Problems With Colonialism

Someone in San Juan sold a tourist a coconut for $25.00 it
should have been enough exotica to last the tourist for a
while but behold when he got to his room in the Caribe
Hilton he came down with electrical diarrhea. He sat down
on the toilet bowl to discharge and when he was through and
reached for the sanitary paper he noticed that there was
none. It had been stolen by the maid who lives in a section
of Bayamón called Fat Back. He was twelve feet away from
the telephone which he was gonna use to call room service
and see what can be done, half way there when he was
between the bed and the chest of drawers the lights went
out, there was a temporary black out affecting that section
San Juan. Goddam Puerto Ricans he said as he reached over
in the dark to the bed and grabbed the blanket and wiped his
butt clean with it, one minute later the lights went back on
and he noticed that he wiped himself with his own white
shirt which he had placed atop the bed moments before
entering the bathroom.

Puerta Rica

Free Puerto Rico
Puerto Rico free
Puerto Rico for $12.50
Puerto Rico on credit
Get some rich port
free
free sand and free soil
Free Puerto Rico now
Give away Puerto Rico
for nothing
Port Rich
Rich Port
Rich free
Port free
Puerto Rico for a
thousand dollars
Free Puerto Rico now
Free Puerto Rico then
Free Puerto Rico always
Puerto Rico on layaway
Puerto Rico as thing
Puerto Rico as word
Puerta Rica
Puerto Rico as blood
as water as gold
Puerto Rico as idea
inside of briefcases
Going to colleges
Puerto Rico patches
Puerto Rico buttons
Puerto Rico as flag
waving
Puerto Rico as in the heart
as in the ocean
The sand as hot as
frying pan
Puerto Rico as lament

Puerto Rico as cement
Puerto Rico as my uncles
house
As Julia Maria
As Borinquen
Going from house to house
In the mountains
for more and more soft
Brown legs
Puerto Rico as the corner
where I stood
And when the sugar cane
trucks went thru town
All that fell down
all you could grab
Was free.

Puerto Rico as
abusement
As absent from your
center of discussion
Puerto Rico as amusement
Puerto Rico free
Puerto Rico as jail
Escape Puerta Rica
like the Maya
Invisible urbanites
take electric
Mayaris
Estudy new ways
not freeways
out of town

Procession

Do you want to know
what the moon is?
The moon is the collected
cut fingernails of all
Past earthly generations
And it is precisely
where it is to scratch
The greatest itch
conceivable.

Root of Three

I walk in New York with a mountain
in my pocket
I walked in Puerto Rico with a guitar
in my belly
I walked in Spain with Mecca
in my sandals
I invented the theory of guayaba
Humacao turned it into a seed
Gave it to a woman
Who dove into a hole in the ground
with it
She came back in seven days
with a round yellow fruit
In Ifa land I was a cane for
the poets of divination
I saw blood cells
moonlight as drum beats

I floated Uranus
When the earth was a sheet of paper
In the book of sparkles
Each ray of light
became a letter
Each letter a mineral
The language of the ocean is turquoise
I noticed this walking to Cidra
From where I took a horse
into Aguas Buenas

I walk New York with a fan
in my pocket
Made with the feathers
of three continents
It blows African feet
It blows Spanish heart
It blows Taíno head space

I am the three in one
The Father
The Son
And the Holy Ghost.

A Skirt in the Distance

Is it only one layer
Closer
Now more layers
silk molasses and bananas
When you thought it was the end of
the pulp
Like a submarine the fingers
separate more cotton
Ruffles
A party and it is only the edge
More thigh
Than Thailand
Windows and escaleras
Cubi holes
Corners

More sugar than Juicy Fruit
Cabinets
Full of cinnamon extraction
Bigger than the horizon
The inclusiveness of her colors
The concentration of the seamstress
The extra touch
Of exaggeration
Needed for the thirst of the dragons
Shape atop shape
Line after line
Untiring amoeba designs
Tenements of lush
Uncrowded
City near her knees
It just goes up the coast

Zig-zags into an amount
Of overwhelming puzzles
Clearing into light
The belly button

and beyond
Soft compositions of flesh
pouring onto the palms
Breaking the coconuts
Sweet liquid of salt
Sugar milk
Everything is in there
More next to more
And weaving.

Caribbean Glances I

Magenta and then bronze
Purple and then cinnamon
Red and then red
White and then mahogany
Pink and then flamingo
Blue and then bolero
Yellow and then love
Green and then blue
Curve and then fragrance
Patcholi and then taste
Mystery and then caves
Wood and then a face
Eyes and then valley
Sorrow and then laughter
Beans and then water
Venus and then tobacco
Night Agua Florida
Morning and birds towards the river
Street and then straw hats
Christ and then everybody
Sunday everyday
Caribbean and then sky.

Is It Certain Or Is It Not Certain Caso Maravilla

Note: In which two young independentistas
        are brutally beaten and killed
        by members of the intelligence division
        Who claimed that they were on their way
        to sabotage a tower which controlled
        the electrical power for the San Juan
        area.

Cover up like mascara
Helena Rubenstein
Not even Paris in its glory
A man has to follow with a sack
To collect objects falling
Given that all objectivity has fallen
The backache is a confusion even
To the Chinese doctor

We're moving with legs down a hill of
what
Listening to a policeman present in the
jam
How he lost his memory
Remembered only that he had a coffee
Two witnesses down another officer
With an I didn't do it kind of face
Said
They had a trail of pork chops
Possibly some rice
And that everyone ate
And the previous police officer
who only recalled coffee
Had seconds according to this
witness
So much for digestion

We are walking up a hill
which is walking down us

Walk in front of Christ
carrying the cross
Pursued by maladies
Chasing the thoughts in your
Mucus head
This is the church people
Of decency repute
The bad people in this case
Are Satanás themselves
Mercy means the opposite
In the dictionary of the lard

Be careful
Cause look what is loose
And possessive of power

If a psychiatrist saw such fantasy
Him make for airport

Christians
Of the kind that sold themselves to Rome
Who maintain the language of the killers
Of Christ
As the ceremonial language of the very
Church of Christ

Condemn them
For they might know what they
are doing
And know no better

Police set them up like dinner table
For Queen Elizabeth
Every knife in its proper place
Saucers and plates at measured angles

Now that you have seen the beauty parlor
imagine the wig

Colonial Spanish language
was directional
Monolingual
A one way street
A question was also an answer
A mind which has nothing to give
Gives it vigorously
Force is what it has learned
From the monarchs
From the priest
Who made a generation of Taínos
transform into biology
to school teachers who teach
you the rules with the very rulers
The plan is to take over
what has been made
While you destroy those
who made it

They kill you one day
The next day they want to know
why are you dead
The Aztecs
The Romans
The armies
The police
Missionaries
who forever want to change beings
Obsessed with others doing something
wrong
This has created a knot
Which not even seven Houdinis
A place in which the devil
screams three times

The search light of the scrambled head
Veins where cheese travels
Watch tower eye head
Those who cannot live life will not
allow anyone else to live it

The plan is to put things in order
To balance the Libras
To put in place
To set straight
To cut to size
To sharpen up
To move out the way
To eliminate
To kill
To invade

Look what a small door
A bull is trying to push
Through dressed as justice
Cerro Maravilla the tall
hill from which everyone must
Run
Senators
Judges
Governor
Desks
Police
Agents
Neck ties
Microphones
Nails
Television
and all

Run into the
Rhythm of justice
Played by the drums of consciousness
Of original mountain rock

We know the proverb well:
You cannot cover the sky with your hands
Especially if the sky is blood red

So be careful
and be cool
Even though
Caquax is hot.

Semanaqua

Semanaqua is sound surrounded by water
Islands of green pensivity
Going and coming rock eternity
We could say the fish started here
Off of Arecibo before it became lyric
Of the popular radio songs of tropical rhythms
Manatí sounds like the place where man
Half fish walked up to the old Mercado
And ate themselves
Looking for Elena the one that told me
She was going to divine village
The village of Manatí
In a car of sea-shells

The espectacular of the day
Was a dinosaur appearing down the street
"O, nothing, just a beast, enroute towards
green salad."
It was of utmost importance to recognize
The carnivorous one
The one that can accommodate your head
into its nostril

Our legs were dancing on the one skull
when it broke into pieces
The shape was made by the movement of the
dancers
The coast has the salt of its lovers
which have left
Never to return again to the old embrace

Eye-sight from the stars
Glitters through the streets
Like Lucifers in the caves

Semanaqua the opposite of a lake

Turns around in her bed
Finds a better position for her sleep
For her play.

Loisaida

By the East River
of Manhattan island
Where once the Iroquois
Canoed in style
Now the jumping
Stretch of Avenue D
housing projects
Where
Rican / Blacks
Johnny Pacheco / Wilson Pickett
Transistor
the radio night
Across the Domino sugar
sign
Red Neon on stage
It's the edge of Brooklyn

From heaven windows
megalopolis light
That's the picture
Into a lizard mind
Below the working
class jumps like frogs
Parrots with new raincoats
Swinging canes of bamboo
Like third legs
Strollers of cool flow
A didy-bop keeping step
time with the finest
Marching through
Red bricks aglow

Hebrew prayers
inside metals
Rolled into walls
Tenement relic
living in Museum
Home driven carts
arrive with the morning
slicing through the
curtains
Along with a Polish
English
Barking peaches and melons
The ice man sells
his hard water
Cut into blocks
Buildings swallowing
coals through their
Basement mouth

Where did the mountains
go
The immigrants ask
The place where houses
and objects went back
In history and entered
The roots of plants
And become eternal again
Now the plaster of Paris
The ears of the walls
The first utterances
in Spanish
Recalled what was left
behind

People kept arriving
as the cane fields dried
They came like flying bushes
from another planet
which had pineapples for moons
Fruits popping out of luggage
The singers of lament

into the soul of Jacob Riis
The Bible tongues
Santa María
Into the Torah
La liturgical lai le lo le
A Spanish never seen
before
Inside the gypsies
Parading through
Warsaw ghetto
Lower East Side
Rabinicals
Begin to vanish
into the economy
Left Loisaida
a skeleton
The works quarter

Orchard Street
garments
Falling off the torso
in motion down the avenue
It seems it could not hold
the cold back

The red Avenue B bus
disappearing down
The drain of Man
Hat on
Dissolving into the
pipes of lower Broadway
The Canals of streets
direct to the factories

After Foresite Park
Is the begining of Italy
Florence inside Mott
Street windows
Palmero eyes of Angie

Criss crossing these
mazes I would arrive
At Loudes home
With knishes she threw
next to red beans

Broome Street Hasidics
with Martian fur hats
Gone with their brims
Puerto Ricans with Pra
Pras
Atop faces with features
thrown out of some bag
Of universal racial
stew
Mississippi sharecroppers
through Avenue D black
Stories
All in exile from broken
Souths
The amapolas the daffodils
were cement tar and steel
Within architectural
gardens remembering
the agriculture of mountain
and field

From the guayava bushels
outside a town with a
Taíno name
I hear a whistle
In the aboriginal ear
With the ancient I
that saw Andalucía
Arrive on a boat
To distribute Moorish
eyes on the coast
Loisaida was faster
than the speed of light
A whirlpool within which

you had to grab on to some-
thing
It took off like a spauldine
hit by a blue broom stick
on 12th street
Winter time summer time
seasons of hallways
And roofs
Between pachanga and duwap
Thousands of Eddies and Carmens
Stars and tyrants
Now gone
From the temporary station of
desire and disaster
The windows sucked them up
The pavement turned out to
be a mouth
Urban vanishment
Illusion
Henry Roth
Call it Sleep.

It's Miller Time

I work for the C.I.A.
They pay me with
cocaine and white Miami
lapel sports jackets
free tickets to San Juan
where I make contact
with a certain bank
official at the Chase
Manhattan Condado branch

My contact a guy named
Pete asks if I know other
accents within the Spanish
Can you sound Salvadorian?
They give me pamphlets
and also send me
pornographic magazines
if I want a stereo or a VCR
they know a place I can
get them at half-price
they told me there is a waiter
that works at Bruno's
who can get me any gadget

The last assignment
I had was to contact
the Public Relations Division
of a beer company
because for U.S. Hispanics
it was Miller Time
I contacted this brewery
a certain Miguel Gone-sa-less
invited me to lunch
I met him at La Fuente
at his suggestion
with him
was Camden New Jersey

Cuban who was going through
town enroute to Los Angeles
the lunch was on them

Señor Gone-sa-less had a
wallet full of plastic
he had more plastic than Woolworth's
they mentioned that the
beer company wanted to sponsor
salsa dance within the Latin
community
bring in the top commercial names
and that while this dance was
going on they wanted to pass
a petition against U.S. involvement
in Central America
they showed me the petition
which had a place for the name and
address of the singers
a great list to have and spread
around all government agencies

They gave a bag with 3 thousand
dollars in it
it was my responsibility to see
this through
the Cuban guy tapped me on the
shoulder and said
Don't have any of the mixed drinks
The bartenders at the dance
are working for us
The chemical people are experimenting
the effects of a liquid
just drink the beer

The festive event went off
successfully even a full moon
was in the sky
next week the CIA is flying me
back to the Caribbean where I
will assist in staging one of

the strangest events in recent history

According to the description in my
orders we are going to pull off a
mock rising of land from beneath
the Caribbean which the media will
quickly identify as lost Atlantis

Circular buildings made of cyrstals
are being constructed somewhere in Texas
they will be part of the spectacle
which will have the world spellbound
simultaneous with this event
the Marines will invade from bases
in Puerto Rico
the countries of Nicaragua
El Salvador and Guatemala
it will be a month of *Salsa*
in San Francisco
an astounding mystical event in the
Caribbean
the price of cocaine coming through
Miami will go down
everybody party and celestial
glittering and drunk
circuits jammed with junk and information

In a daze the world is free
for Miller Time.

The Face Without Makeup

Pictograph this:
If we awoke one day
lets say tomorrow
And all the water in the
oceans was gone
I mean every last drop
The bed of the oceans
remaining not even
Moist
That whole world visible
for eye y telescope
Binoculars catch
The sight of thousands
and thousands of tons
of fish drying
Jumping doing the
Jerk
Octopus and whale
Shark and sardine
Down there dry
Taking sun
Lying as if in a
Fish market—
Then you see that
the earth is not round
That it is more like clay
fashioned by Salvador Dali.

Hurakan

Control yourself
be a gentle breeze
As the East Trade winds
So many times you have
taken the hat off
Our heads
Here we give you fruits
mangos
And sweet bananas
We give you our hands of
flesh
We give you our mountain tops
to comb
But slowly and with style
Don't come down with violent
brush
For there are children asleep
Why have you pulled our hair
in such rush
Why do you growl like a dragon
your deep impersonal breath
Why do you bring water
to baptize us in such a
murderous rage
Are we not your children
whom you guided from the stars
To fall in a tropical garden
and out of salt made our lips
That now sing a hymn to you
Father mother of this planet
Red
Still you are hungry and have
eaten us in Mexico and Ponce
God of earth and wind
Take these sweet bodies
For we must be the best food
Sons of guitar and drums

You see the flowers without eyes
Come swallow us
we are cured in spices
Mountain of barrio Mamayes
Opened its mouth and ate
The shanty town
Its lamentations and dreams
its plena rhythms of pena
Come on and eat us all now
God of earth quakes
God of wind
Take back your bones
Cause we are not gonna move
We will shine bones
And place them all together
Until we make a floor with them
From Ponce and Mexico back
towards the sea
And dance upon them
When the sun comes up
Again

Recognizing Cod Fish

If our olfactory level is not
focused
We will suffer its presense
without awareness
A package and a cage complete
with a massage of beauty
Embroidery crismon silk
In that basin of mud we
march stuck to the knees
There you are surrounded by
walls made of crushed pork
Chop bone

You are in the jail of
ridicule
The guard is a stench
Your nose on vacation
in high air
If you get a glimpse
of one jumping out of the
Water at a distance from
the shore of your life
It should wanna make you
run
Towards a saintly shower
of firm determinations
When cod starts talking
recognize the verse of the fish
The melodious harmony that
exploits your heart
Cod fish hearts are made of
card board
And children should draw in
them
The honest truth with the
shape of love

But what is cod in its deepest
sea?
An invention of the Devil
his horns mixing the stew
It is the failure of recognition
to ignite the moment the smoke
Bomb goes off—
Or of the foot not to step
on the suggestion of the drum
To be in Cape Cod is one thing
Then not to know it increases
to another

At the market recognize the boned
from the boneless
On the street note when it is in
costume, in disguise
For cod fish is the world of the
lie
Deception on its wings
The birth place of purist
stink
Cod fish
Amazing
Breathes out of the water
Be up with the light
Other wise submit into the
Pot and simmer within the
guise.